Mama Ethel's Guide

to L♥VE

and
Healthy Relationships

Ethel M. Chadwick

God bless you!

Ethel Chadwick ☺

Mama Ethel's Guide

to L♥VE

and Healthy Relationships

Ethel M. Chadwick

MAMA ETHEL'S GUIDE TO LOVE
and Healthy Relationships

Printed in the USA

ISBN 978-1-941173-58-9

1. 2. 3.

Published by

Olive **P**ress Messianic and Christian Publisher
www.olivepresspublisher.com
olivepressbooks@gmail.com

Messianic & Christian Publisher

Our prayer at Olive Press is that we may help make the Word of Adonai fully known, that it spread rapidly and be glorified everywhere. We hope our books help open people's eyes so they will turn from darkness to Light and from the power of the adversary to God and to trust in יֵשׁוּעַ Yeshua (Jesus). (From II Thess. 3:1; Col. 1:25; Acts 26:18,15 NRSV and CJB) .

Dedication

This book is dedicated to my dear husband Daniel, who has always believed in me, encouraged me, and taught me how to love and trust again, and to my children and grandchildren, who are the joy of my heart, and the spark in my eye. The Lord has blessed me greatly and I am truly thankful!

[God's Perfect] Love
is patient; *Love* is kind;
Love is not envious,
boastful, arrogant or rude.
It does not insist on its
own way; it is not irritable
or resentful.
Love never fails.
And now faith, hope, *Love,*
...the greatest of these is
Love.

I Cor. 13:4-5, 8,13 (loosely NRSV)

**Now (we) know only in part,
then (we) will know fully....**
I Cor. 13:12b (NRSV)

Therefore

encourage one another

and

build **each other**

up....

I Thess. 5:11

Endorsements

When Ethel Chadwick asked me to write this endorsement for her book, a warm smile came to my face when I saw the book title, *Mama Ethel's Guide to Love and Healthy Relationships*. Having known Ethel for many years, the title so epitomized this upbeat, vivacious, and gregarious lady.

The book you hold in your hand is filled with practical wisdom borne of many years of experience. In life, our best learning comes from the proverbial "school of hard knocks."

When I first met Ethel in the mid 80's, she was in the throes of deep crisis as she found herself having to rear three young children by herself. The going was tough but through the strength of the Lord she was able to climb above the pain and heartaches she endured.

The Holy One of Israel heard and answered the cries of her heart through her soon-to-be husband Daniel, a quiet soft spoken, scholarly man with a good sense of humor and a heart of gold.

Mama Ethel's Guide to Love and Healthy Relationships is more than just a wisdom writing on the topic of relationships but is also a personal testimony of His faithfulness! This work is truly a labor of love and I find myself thankful to have had a front row seat to witness this great testimony.

Most sincerely,
Rabbi Frank Lowinger
Congregation Brith Hadoshah, Buffalo, NY

Mama Ethel's Guide to Love and Healthy Relationships is like sitting with your best friend over coffee and having a long chat about what's on your heart. Ethel writes in a very conversational manner, inviting the reader to consider some of the nuggets of wisdom she has collected in her walk as a Jewish believer, and wife and mother.

This little volume is filled with good reminders from Scripture, which she interweaves into the text, about how to deal with various relational situations. Ethel doesn't shy away from sharing her own vulnerabilities and mistakes which make what she has to say all the more accessible. Her honesty and transparency are refreshing. For those of us who struggle with some or many of our relationships, which is generally most of us, "Mama Ethel's Guide..." is a warm and friendly reminder of the need to see each other through the lens of God's love.

Shalom,
Sally Klein Oconnor
Messianic recording artist

Reading *Mama Ethel's Guide to Love and Healthy Relationships* is like visiting the sweet but unambiguous neighbor next door for coffee and a bit of advice. Ethel Chadwick's book flows like a conversation; unpretentious, loving, wise, considerate, and full of advice - if you'll listen. Never pushy and with years of life experience, she skillfully weaves scripture into her own stories and others, causing her readers to come away with a sense of belonging, safety, hope, understanding, and inspiration! So, put on a pot of tea, curl up in your favorite chair, and remind yourself through her words that God loves you and He has a wonderful journey ahead for your life. His principles are tried and true and conveyed so beautifully in this short, poignant, consultation with a Jewish mama!

Corry Keeler
Worship Leader, International Recording Artist,
    and Director of Lev Shelo Ministries

Ethel Chadwick's uplifting book *Mama Ethel's Guide to Love and Healthy Relationships* is full of wise, practical, and spiritual guidance, leading the reader to godly choices in every sphere of human interaction. Ethel's sage advice about communication, humility and grace, peace, and the importance of genuine love—among other topics—is user friendly and adaptable to various life situations. The examples and illustrations are combined with a generous mix of directness and humor that makes it all go down smoothly. Ethel finishes this important work with her wonderful Messianic Jewish testimony.

Please take some time to check out this enjoyable book. You'll be glad you did.

Rabbi Michael Wolf
Author of *The Upper Zoo* and the *Linotype* series.

Mama Ethel's Guide to Love and Healthy Relationships is a must-read! First of all, because it is written by my charming, delightful, clever friend, Ethel. But also because it's full of sound, biblical advice on how to build a strong, healthy, happy marriage.

Ethel's writing style is honest, approachable, and pragmatic without being preachy. You will appreciate Ethel's folksy, matter-of-fact, and sometimes raw presentation.

There is a chapter about listening, a chapter about forgiveness, and even a chapter about how to disagree with one's spouse respectfully and lovingly. Ethel's wise counsel is punctuated with humor, honesty, scripture, and real-life experience. Plus, she plainly and frequently points to Yeshua, His words, His teachings, and His ways. I especially appreciate Ethel's emphasis on repentance, humility, and submission in our marriages and in all our relationships. I can't imagine a successful marriage without these!

I believe this book would be an invaluable resource for any married or betrothed couple. It contains foundational content for those who are engaged to be married, (in fact, I know a couple I would love to purchase it for!) And Ethel's wisdom is also a powerful and important refresher for those of us who've been happily married for years. Even unmarried folks would benefit from reading this, as there are chapters that deal with how to prayerfully and patiently wait for "the one" to come along.

I'm honored to highly recommend *Mama Ethel's Guide to Love and Healthy Relationships*.

Sue Samuel
Messianic Worship Leader/Recording Artist

Mama Ethel's Guide to Love by Ethel Chadwick is a beautiful and easy to read book on how to find and maintain healthy relationships, and how to recover from broken ones. Her writing deals with very significant, relationship and heart issues and yet manages to be enjoyable to read. Ethel's personal struggles with relationships are shared with genuine transparency which helps to make the content very absorbing. I highly recommend this book for everyone because we all need Ethel's well explained insights to deal with all our relationships.

Rabbi Jim Appel
Congregation Shema Yisrael
Rochester, New York

Bagels, Blessings, and Books

It occurred to me, as I pondered what to say about our friend, Ethel Chadwick, and her new book—that she is the perfect person to expound on matters meaningful and Messianic and to encourage and enhance our spiritual lives.

Ethel is a faithful and devoted follower of her Messiah, Yeshua, an impassioned evangelist for His kingdom—(which is now and is to come)—and an excellent and exuberant host of "Bagels and Blessings," a show featuring interviews, information and insights, not only from her own unique perspective but also from the viewpoints of many others who follow Yeshua and seek to live for Him.

However, to me, what commends her most as an ambassador, a commentator and an author for the Lord is her role—and her calling—as a Mom—and a Jewish one, at that!

It tickled me to think that all of creation has, as it's eternal sovereign, the Jewish Son of a Jewish mom!

He is—and will ever be—the head over a household rightly deemed a "mishpachah"—a family.

That is what the God of Israel wants us all—Jew and non-

Endorsements (cont.)

Jew alike—to be; sons and daughters of one Father, loving each other as He loves us.

There is no one more qualified to share her life in the Lord with yours than this Jewish mother who loves the blessed and divine Son of another Jewish mother—and has dedicated her life to caring for the family birthed in His Name.

So why don't you toast a bagel, take a seat at Ethel's table and receive a blessing from what she has to offer.

Enjoy!!

Marty Goetz Ministries/House Of Worship
Messianic Music Minister

Foreword

The world is full of so many different people, it can boggle your mind. To think that in this vast diversity there could only be two souls that fit together is dangerous at worst and naive at best. The idea implies that choice isn't important nor hard work normal.

Great relationships don't happen by accident. Sure, there are some people you just click better with. But being afraid or lazy in relationships means you don't value someone enough to fight for them (or even yourself). At the first sign of tension, do you push away or press in?

I might be the only person on the planet that loves this obscure Proverb but I am convinced it describes relationships.

"The only clean stable is an empty stable. So if you want the work of an ox and to enjoy an abundant harvest, you'll have a mess or two to clean up!" (Proverbs 14:4 TPT).

When we let people close to us, things can get messy. Emotions can be complex. Fear is blinding and insecurity, a thief. But the reward that awaits us for not giving up, for seeking understanding and filling our hearts and homes with deep connection is worth it. I've seen Mama Ethel manifest this truth in her life.

Through the hardest times and in the face of pain, I have seen her press forward and refuse to give up, all with a smile on her face and a warm hand to lead us forward. There is much increase if we're willing to press in, not push away. And that's what *Mama Ethel's Guide to Love and Healthy Relationships* is—it's the reins to help us press forward and an invitation to get a little messy for the gems in our lives that are truly worth it.

J. Kelley (Wife, Mother,
Daughter of Mama Ethel, Amateur Writer,
Coffee Enthusiast, Engineer and Manager).

Table Of Contents

Endorsements   9

Foreword   14

Dear Readers   19

1. New Chances   21

2. Love Your Neighbor As Yourself
     Don't Take Things Personally   25

3. How Do You Know?   29

4 Patience in Waiting   . 35

5. Is Anybody Listening?   41

6. We Teach Others How to Treat Us   45

7. Choose Your Battles   49

8. That Nasty Thing Called Pride   53

9. Stop Trying to Fix People   57

10. Hold Onto the Word   63

11. Forgiveness   69

12. Triggers   77

13 When You Disagree   81

14. Know You Are Loved and Act Accordingly   85

15. You are Beautiful   91

16. Please and Thank You   95

17. Perfect Love Drives Out Fear   101

18. The Power of Hugs   109

19. Let's Do Lunch   113

20. Just Friends   117

21. The Conclusion of Mama Ethel's
     Marriage Advice   121

22. My Testimony   125

About the Author   131

"I've always been a romantic at heart."

Mama Ethel

Dear Readers,

I hope you come to think of me as your friend, your sister, perhaps even a "mother" figure in your life. While I'm not terribly old compared to some, let's just say I've been around the block a few times, and have experienced many of the same things you experience on a daily basis: fear, anxiety, restlessness, self-rejection, bitterness and hopelessness.

In this book we'll explore many of these things — some of my thoughts will be random, some will speak straight into your soul and others will be — let's just say — ridiculous and seemingly pointless.

You see, I've always been a romantic at heart. My favorite movies are the ones where the guy gets the girl, they live happily ever after, having a wonderful life together. Of course the reality is staggering, not all relationships turn out that way. Well, if I can have any part in saving relationships, steering couples in the right direction, and helping them communicate and grow old together, I'm going to do my best! I admit, growing up, I didn't date a lot, and my first marriage didn't work out, but somehow, I learned a whole lot along the way. I want to share a few things from my heart, so grab a cup of coffee and indulge me, won't you? I may not be an expert, but I know a few things.

By the way, I am a Messianic Jew and have used the Hebrew name for Jesus, "Yeshua," throughout the book.

Let's get started!
Mama Ethel

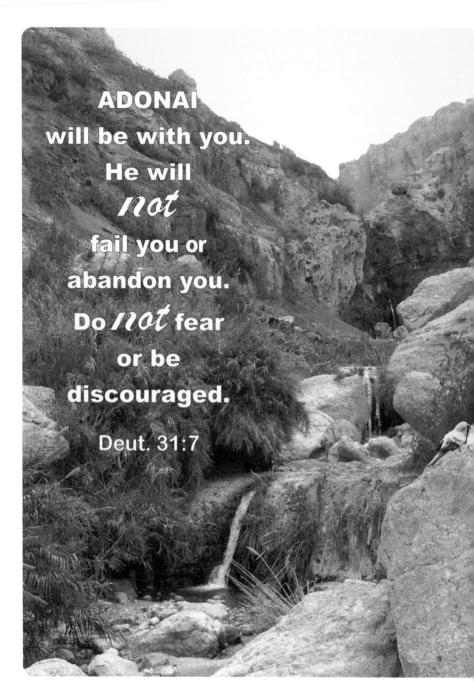

ADONAI
will be with you.
He will
not
fail you or
abandon you.
Do *not* fear
or be
discouraged.

Deut. 31:7

20

CHAPTER ONE

New Chances

Happy New Year everyone! (It may not be near New Year's Day when you are reading this book, but it was when I wrote this chapter, so please play along with me. Okay?) So here we are at that place where we decide to do it all differently. We make resolutions, we plan to lose 20 pounds, spend less time on Facebook, eat more fiber, and we vow never to drive over the speed limit again.

But what happens when we don't keep our promises to ourselves? We grow despondent. We become bitter and resentful, and sometimes we just lose hope.

OK, stop right there. Did you forget that the Bible says that His mercies are new every morning? Yep, it says so right in Lamentations 3:22-23. Have you ever heard of that expression "just take baby steps"?

Each day, all you can do is your best. Give it your best effort. If you are overly critical and unforgiving of yourself, chances are that you are also this way in your relationships. If your sweetie forgets to skip that extra cookie are you going to pounce on him and make him feel bad? There is a right way and a wrong way to encourage someone to take better care of themselves. It's usually best to talk to him in private and never publicly—no one wants to be publicly humiliated.

What works best with you? Would you rather someone yelled into your face (similar to what they do in the Marines) and told you that you were useless and stupid each time you messed up? Or would you rather someone gently reminded you (in private) and loved you through it?

That's what I'm talking about. When you make a mistake, you have to forgive yourself and hear the voice of Yeshua gently encouraging you to do better next time.

Each morning when you wake up, you have a choice. You can dwell on your past mistakes or you can try to do things differently. The good news is that you are not alone! As you get deeper into the Word, you will see so many loving scriptures reminding you that the Lord will never leave you. Deuteronomy 31:8 says "ADONAI—He is the One who goes before you. He will be with you. He will not fail you or abandon you. Do not fear or be discouraged."

If you are kinder to yourself, you will be kinder to others. I'm sure you have met people who project their self-anger onto others. They are not very happy people and make others very upset by being overly critical. If you recognize yourself here, then please pray and ask the Lord to help you in this area. When you love and accept yourself, you are more likely to be more tolerant of others.

New Chances

Some good New Year's Resolutions would be to start each day with prayer, spend more time in the Word, be kinder and more forgiving to yourself and to others, and strive to share the Good News of Yeshua whenever possible. I'm sure you can think of others.

Now, about speeding. Hmm, notice I didn't mention that one? Yes, Mama Ethel has a few weaknesses of her own and will be seeking the Lord about this. You may wish to pray about that!

Some of my own resolutions, in addition to the ones above, would be to hug more people, laugh more, sing and dance more, and listen more than talk!

In case you wondered, I haven't forgotten that we Jews celebrate the New Year in the fall on Rosh Hashanah, but we do live in this world and when the calendar rolls over from December to January there is always a bit of excitement, don't you think?

May the Lord bless you abundantly and give you the desires of your heart! This is the year of ADONAI's favor! (Isaiah 61:2)

Shalom,
Mama Ethel

Love your neighbor as yourself
Matt. 22:39

I praise You,
for I am

*awesomely,
wonderfully*

made!

Psalm 139:14

Chapter Two

Love Your Neighbor as Yourself, and Don't Take Things Personally

Let's explore the Scripture "Love your neighbor as yourself" (Matthew 22:39; Mark 12:31). I know, you've heard this phrase your whole life, blah blah blah.....

But what does it really mean?

During my college years I read Erich Fromm's book, *The Art of Loving*,[1] and earned an "A" in English for writing a paper on it. The book totally lines up with Scripture when you think about it—because the whole point of Mr. Fromm's book is that you cannot fully love another person until you love yourself!

I know what you are thinking—"easier said than done." How do you love yourself when you never received love and affirmation when you were young? What if you never received encouragement or praise, what if no one ever hugged you? I know, it's kind of

1 Harper & Row 1956, Harper Perennial Modern Classic 2006.

hard to suddenly love yourself and feel really good about your life when you have faced opposition and criticism every step of the way.

And I also know you can't just turn on a switch and suddenly appreciate yourself. But here's something I want you to think about. The God of Abraham, Isaac and Jacob, the same God who created the universe— He sees you! And not only does He see you, He thinks you are pretty special! How do I know this? Well, I'm not going to start spitting out hundreds of Scriptures. I do like this psalm very much though: Psalm 139:13-18. Basically, it says that God knew you before you were formed in the womb, all your days were written in His book AND you are awesomely and wonderfully made!

Of course, there are hundreds of passages in the Bible that affirm His love for you. My dear friend in Messiah, if you could just see yourself as He sees you. If you could just realize that you are wonderful and fantastic and that He has a plan for your life. If you could begin to look in the mirror and see the beauty in your eyes. If you could let His love flow into you and through you—then you just might begin to really love yourself!

And guess what? When you get to that place of loving yourself, and are really at peace with who you are, and you understand that there is a plan for your life, then and only then are you truly ready to be in a loving relationship with another person!

We hear a lot about dysfunction and co-dependency. I will address these issues in Chapter 9. Suffice it to say here that until you love yourself and see yourself as Abba Father sees you, most of your relationships will, in fact, be dysfunctional and co-dependent.

When you're secure in who you are in Messiah and walk in the confidence that He gives you, then you are less likely to take things personally!

I know many of you have read the book, _The Four Agreements_.[2] While I certainly do not endorse some of the new age philosophy prevalent in that book, the ideas presented are good ones. The agreement, that mattered the most to me was "don't take anything personally." This is very difficult but so liberating! When someone is upset or rude to you, don't take it personally! When someone is not friendly at synagogue or if someone forgets to call you or write you back, don't take it personally!!! Most of the time the person has his or her own issues, and it has NOTHING TO DO WITH YOU!

As you become more "God-centered" and less "self-centered," you will stop taking things personally! This will greatly benefit all your relationships.

I am blessed to have many friends, a loving husband, and three wonderful adult children. We've had our ups and downs. We've had to learn and relearn to respect each other's boundaries, and we're still learning and growing.

That's what life is all about—learning and growing, as the Lord leads. Be blessed and remember, every day of your life is an opportunity to be a blessing to someone!

Mama Ethel

---

2 Don Miguel Ruiz, _The Four Agreements: A Practical Guide to Personal Freedom_ (A Toltec Wisdom Book), Amber-Allen Publishing, 1997.

Delight
yourself
in *Adonai,*
and He will
give **you**
the requests
of your heart.

Psalm 37:4

Chapter Three

How Do You Know?

I love interviewing couples to find out their story—how they met, which one made the first move, what their first impression was, etc. Then I always ask, "How did you know that he or she was THE ONE?"

Every story is different, and some stories are more "flavorful" than others, but there are always some common threads.

For those couples who are believers in Yeshua, they usually tell me that they have been praying about their future mate for a very long time. Most have made a list of special qualities that they hope to find. At the top of the list is "dedication to the Lord." The next qualities vary from person to person, but here are some common traits:

- Has a good sense of humor
- Is a good listener (not so eager to talk about themselves)
- Is good with children
- Is good with finances, financially stable
- Is willing to work
- Has self control, gentleness

- Is humble
- Is creative (art, music, etc)
- Has a love of travel, adventure
- Is willing to take risks
- Is willing to share household tasks

These are just a few of the qualities I know people are hoping to find, and obviously some are more important than others. I heard a funny story once: a lady took a pair of men's trousers, hung them on her bedpost and said, "Lord, fill those pants!!" Waiting can be the hardest part. Some people find their life partner at sixteen years of age, while others may not meet that special person until they are forty years old.

Please be encouraged that our God has perfect timing (Ecclesiastes 3) and wants to give you the requests of your heart (Psalm 37:4). While you are waiting, try to stay focused—be a blessing to your neighbors, your colleagues at work, and, of course, to your family members. Join a bowling league, attend art exhibits, volunteer at the hospital and at your congregation, of course. Go out with friends, take a class at the community college or even at the Red Cross. Embrace Jury Duty, as it's also an opportunity to meet people you normally wouldn't meet. Let your light shine at all times, reflect His goodness. Remember to seek the Lord first (Matthew 6:33), and all these things will be added unto you!

What are some red flags? Well, first let me remind you that the perfect person isn't out there. Be sure you have reasonable expectations. Having said that, I have another list for you. Remember, this is just my opinion. You can disagree and that's perfectly alright. I would avoid someone with these qualities:

- Talks about him/herself too much
- Doesn't listen well
- Dwells on the past
- Gets angry easily
- Holds a grudge – doesn't forgive
- Doesn't encourage you
- Finds fault, criticizes often
- Needs constant reassurance, needy, too insecure
- Doesn't trust you
- Doesn't respect your choices
- Needs constant attention, smothering
- Has self-hatred, is self condemning
- Is fearful of everything
- Has no faith in God, never prays
- Swears like a sailor
- Is addicted to drugs, alcohol, gambling
- Is too eager for sexual intimacy
- Doesn't respect your boundaries

I am sure you can come up with a whole lot more. These are just a few things that came into my head. Remember, dear friends, you should never enter a relationship hoping that the other person will change. You can certainly pray that they will improve, grow stronger, more confident, etc., but hoping that they will be something entirely different isn't fair and is harmful to the relationship.

Be patient and trust God that He will find the right person. Don't ever settle!

Please know that when you meet the one that God has intended for you, you'll know deep in your heart that this is the one. I believe the Lord will give you supernatural peace that surpasses all understanding. It's much more than just butterflies and physical attraction—it's a feeling, deep in your soul. You'll know that you know.

By the way, some readers of this book feel called to be single, and that's certainly acceptable to me. I'm simply addressing those who are still waiting to meet their special someone.

I hope I have encouraged you if even just a little. I was very blessed to find love again as a single parent with three young children. It took a very special man to love not only me, but also my children. Our God is that big—so even if you are divorced with children, you can still find love. With God all things are possible (Matthew 19:26)!

I don't know why it takes so long sometimes. I just know that it's always worth the wait. Please don't give in to fear and anxiety. "Perfect love drives out fear" (1 John 4:18). Trust that the Lord is in control. And be ready! Look up, be expectant, and keep smiling!!

Mama Ethel

For I *know* the plans that
I have in mind for you,"
declares Adonai,
"plans for *shalom* and
not calamity—
to give you a future and a
hope.

Jeremiah 29:11

Chapter Four

Patience in Waiting

Did you ever hear the one about praying for patience? The moment you pray for it, you get a challenge—or so they say! We hear a lot about God's timetable. We know that, according to Jeremiah 29:11, He has a purpose and a plan for our life. We read in Ecclesiastes 3 that there is a time and a season for everything. And we hear stories from our friends about the benefits of waiting.

Waiting seems to be one of the hardest things we do. Whether you're waiting for a job promotion, an offer on your house, or for God to bring you a spouse, you will be challenged to trust and stay firm in your faith.

No one ever said it was easy. The question is how long do you think you can wait? If you knew that God was going to give you far beyond what you desired, wouldn't it be worth the wait? What can you do while you're waiting? Is there a way to speed up the process?

Since my book deals mainly with relationships, let's focus on waiting for God to bring you a spouse. Some of you have been waiting for many years and are discouraged, frustrated, lonely, and depressed.

I do believe that God has perfect timing, but I also believe that we can be proactive. As mentioned before, sometimes this means that we change part of our routine—we enroll in a class, join a bowling league, go to a conference, volunteer at a soup kitchen, join a ministry at our congregation, etc. I think you get the idea. Believers are everywhere; you just need to keep your ears and eyes open.

I also suggest that you smile often. Really! People are attracted to warm, positive people. Practice good listening skills, show compassion and kindness often, and reflect Yeshua's love in all your interactions.

Just as no man knows the hour when Yeshua returns, we don't know when God will put that special someone in your path. Stay close to the Word, praise Him daily, and do not give in to fear, anxiety, and worry, no matter how long it takes. Expect God to bless you and know that He's got this!

While I'm on the subject, I also know that sometimes God can use on-line dating services to help you meet the right person. There has been some debate over whether or not this is "kosher." Mama Ethel's view is that God can use many different methods to answer our prayers. I would suggest that you pray about it and perhaps discuss it with your Rabbi or Pastor, and if you have peace about it, then I would go ahead. There are Messianic dating sites as well as mainstream Christian sites, and I do not know which ones are better. I am sure you can ask around or Google one of them to see success rates, etc.

Most importantly, pray hard! I would also suggest that you keep a journal. Write down the qualities you look for in a mate, and begin praying for your spouse—and pray that you will be the answer to someone else's prayer as well!

As a single mother of two toddlers and a baby, after a long, bumpy wait full of disappointment and heartbreak, I wrote in my journal that I was tired of one-sided relationships, and I asked God to please give me a relationship where someone pursues me. About a month later, I got a surprise phone call.

A man I had met at a local Bible study called me and said, "Would you consider going out with me sometime?" It was Daniel.

I was so shocked that without thinking, I blurted out, "Well, I wouldn't exactly be repulsed."

I don't recommend that kind of response, of course, but amazingly it didn't deter him. He persistently pursued me and fell deeply in love with me. He even loved my little darlings. We have now been married for 35 years, and he has been a most wonderful, loving husband and father, and is now an amazing grandfather.

Remember, God knows your heart. He knows your desires. In the meantime, get together with friends, attend Bible studies, go to concerts, and enjoy the friends that God has given you.

Sometimes God has us wait because we're still growing. While we may think we're ready, more preparation is needed. We're being refined, renewed, and changed daily, and only He knows when we're ready for the next phase. I know it's hard to wait. Trust me, it will be worth it. I wish I could tell you how much longer. It could be a month, a year, even five years. Only God knows. Do you trust Him? It will be worth the wait. "But seek first the kingdom of God and His righteousness, and all these things shall be added to you." – Matthew 6:33. Hang in there, my dear!

Mama Ethel

So in all things,
do to *others*
what you
would want
them
to do to you.

Matt. 7:12

Chapter Five

Is Anybody Listening?

Shalom my friends! Let's talk about listening! We all love it when someone leans forward, looks into our eyes, and dotes on our every word—right? Unfortunately, in our busy society with all the chores, obligations, and distractions, we don't always do well with this one. As we explore ways to have better relationships with our loved ones, I am reminded that the best relationships are ones where great listening skills are consistently demonstrated.

Remember Ecclesiastes the 3rd chapter? It's all about timing. When your husband comes home after a hard day at the office, maybe that's not the best time to start a lengthy conversation where you share all your hopes and dreams. If your wife just walked into the door after a five-day conference, maybe you'd better hold off showing her the mistake in the electric bill.

Prayer can really be a blessing when it comes to timing because God wants us to be at peace. We can pray—not only about what to say and how to say it, but about WHEN to say it. God really does have perfect timing—that's a fact!

We're talking about communicating, sharing something important with our friends and family. So after we've prayed, and we believe it's a good time, how do we begin? If we have to mention an area of improvement or a criticism of any kind, it's important to use the "sandwich" approach. Start out with something positive, mention areas that need improvement, and end with more positive, encouraging words. It's a formula used by executives all over the world, and is known to be effective. Try not to use statements that begin with "you," but rather use sentences that begin with, "When you do_____, sometimes it makes me feel _____."

Don't bring up the past—that's really not nice. When we bring up the past, it shows that we are carrying grudges and that we haven't forgiven. It usually makes the other person feel badly about themselves.

As believers in Yeshua, we are encouraged to hold each other up, to be sensitive to each other's needs, and to demonstrate the gifts of the Spirit. Gal. 5:22-23 "But the fruit of the *Ruach* (Spirit) is love, joy, peace, patience, kindness, goodness, faithfulness, gentleness, and self-control." Remember the golden rule! We are to treat others as we would like to be treated.

Now let's talk about listening. When your friends and loved ones speak to you, they really do need to know that they have your full attention. If you are constantly checking your phone or you keep glancing down to continue what you were reading, that sends the message that something else is more important. Take out your ear buds. Put down your book, tablet, phone, or newspaper, and look him or her in the eye.

Occasionally lean forward, nod your head, and be sure to show compassion and empathy.

This next part is often more for guys than gals, but we're all in need of a good reminder. Don't offer advice unless you have permission. Many times your loved one just needs to vent and really doesn't want advice. If asked, you can state your opinion. However, in most cases, you just need to offer your strong shoulder, hold a hand, or give a hug. I know how hard this is for some folks—cause you want to fix a problem immediately. If you are asked to help fix it, go for it. But if not, remember, they just want you to listen. They just need to vent! (Maybe I should pray for patience for you!)

Sometimes you might feel like you've been attacked. Whoa pardner! This is where reflective listening skills are needed. You can say, "So what I hear you saying is that sometimes I........" It's so important to show the other person that you heard them. This takes practice. You might want to get together with a friend and take turns speaking and reflecting back what you heard. You might be surprised how seldom we do this, and it's really a wonderful and helpful tool. When you reflect their words back to them, it has a calming, disarming affect. They feel terrific—like somebody finally gets them!

This is only the tip of the iceberg. It's not always easy to be a good listener. We have so many things on our minds, and it's so easy to be distracted. Ask the Lord to help you communicate better—with love, gentleness, and encouragement, and ask Him to make you a better listener. You can do all things through Messiah who strengthens you (Philippians 4:13)!

Mama Ethel

For **ADONAI**
is *good.*
His lovingkindness
endures *forever,*
and
His faithfulness
to *all* generations

Psalm 100:5

Chapter Six

We Teach Others How to Treat Us

Eleanor Roosevelt is credited with saying, "No one can make you feel inferior without your consent." My dear friends, by now, from you reading this book, I have reminded you once and will a couple more times that the Lord loves you, that the Scriptures say you are "awesomely, wonderfully made" (Psalm 139:14), and that the Bible is full of promises that show you how precious you are in His eyes.

When you see yourself as God sees you, then you are able to have self-respect, which will attract positive people to you.

People often ask how it is possible that some folks allow themselves to be mistreated. One answer is that sometimes people have such low self-esteem, that they are filled with loathing and self-hatred, and may feel that they deserve to be treated poorly.

Another answer is that often people who have been abused have become so used to their situation that they gravitate toward abusive relationships because it's all they have known. Being treated kindly and lovingly is so foreign to them that they are subconsciously drawn to what feels familiar.

If this describes your feelings about yourself, my heart goes out to you, dear one. I hope you can find a way to escape from abuse to a safe place.

Sometimes you need to separate from someone who is abusing you. If you or your family are being threatened, you need to leave immediately, get to safety (a friend or family's home or a shelter), and call the police!

The important thing to remember is that you do not deserve to be treated badly. You are a child of the King and are precious! You are not alone. Let your friends and family help you because they love you very much and will be praying for you.

The enemy has been lying to you. Please take a moment to renounce that lying spirit of self-hatred in Yeshua's Name and repent for allowing it to grow in your mind and heart. Renounce, resist, and remove this spirit in the Name of Yeshua. Replace those thoughts with the Word of God, with Scriptures like Psalm 100:5 "For ADONAI is good. His lovingkindness endures forever, and His faithfulness to all generations" or Psalm 139:14, quoted above. Each time you start to have these thoughts, you must stop yourself and replace them with the Word of God.

There are wonderful organizations that can help you get to safety and survive and heal. May the Lord lead you to the right one for you. Check out giveherwings.com, hurtbylove.com, calledtopeace.org, wildernesstowild.

com, honorprojectmovement.org, and psalm82initiative. org.

Brothers and sisters in Messiah, when you feel good about yourself, you do not allow anyone to take advantage of you. When you are filled with confidence and know who you are in Yeshua, you stand tall, and you do not, under any circumstances, tolerate abuse of any kind.

We all need these reminders. As we learn to see ourselves as God sees us, as we learn to respect ourselves, we will occasionally need to say, "You may not speak to me this way," or "You may not treat me like that" to someone who is treating us badly.

Nehemiah 8:10 says "The joy of ADONAI is your strength." I love this Scripture because I love being filled with joy and walking in His strength.

So choose your friends wisely and associate with those who are like-minded and will lift you up. Stay away from those who bring you down. There is too much negativity in the world today and we don't have to be like them (Romans 12:2).

Bottom line—you deserve to be treated with respect, to be honored, cherished, and nurtured. Stand tall, hold your head up high, and teach others the right way to treat you by treating yourself well.

Mama Ethel

**Be angry,
but don't sin—**

**don't let the
sun go down
before you have
dealt with
the cause of
your anger.**

Ephesians 4:26 (CJB)

Chapter Seven

Choose Your Battles

Did you ever walk into a movie theater knowing that you would absolutely love what you were about to see—or were you dragged in kicking and screaming because you just knew you'd hate it? You already had it all planned out, didn't ya?

I once heard an amazing quote—"expectations are planned resentments." Wow, that's something to think about! I'm not saying we should never expect anything fabulous when in a relationship, but think about how many times you are setting yourself up to get mad at someone when you don't get what you want, or they don't meet your needs exactly as you had planned. Remember, everyone has a different love language, and your spouse may communicate love to you differently than what you were expecting (*The Five Love Languages* by Gary Chapman).[3]

You might be the kind of person that writes post-it notes all over the house to show your affection, and if your honey doesn't respond in kind, resentment can

3 *The Five Love Languages: The Secret to Love That Lasts*, Northfield Publishing, Chicago, 1992, 1995, 2004, 2010, 2015.

start festering. Or maybe you're the kind of person that makes reservations weeks in advance, but your sweetie just likes to be spontaneous.

Don't get me wrong. I'm not the relationship expert, and I'm not saying I have a perfect marriage. But after 35 years with the same person, I have learned a few things along the way.

One thing I have learned is how easy it is to get mad at my husband. Sometimes I forget that it's more important to put his needs first, and if by chance he forgets to pick up blueberries at the store, it doesn't mean he doesn't love me. If he decides to stay home when I want him to go with me to a wedding, I can nag, whine, lay on the guilt, sulk, etc., OR I can accept his decision and let him stay home. That's really a win-win for both of us. I don't resent him for not going, and he isn't badgered into doing something he doesn't want to do. And when I stop and think about it, there were many times when he DID go with me to events, and I need to remember that.

The Lord is so gracious and gentle with me, and if you seek Him, He will help you also. It's so important to choose your battles. It's too easy to get mad and let resentment build up. Ephesians 4:26 (CJB) says, "Be angry, but don't sin—don't let the sun go down before you have dealt with the cause of your anger." If we have resentment and anger towards our spouse or boyfriend or girlfriend, we need to take responsibility for it, confess it and repent of it to the Lord, and re-nounce, resist, and rebuke it in the Name of Yeshua!

Then we need to remove it and all its spiritual roots in Yeshua's Name and replace it with forgiveness, patience, and God's perfect love that comes from continually being refilled with the Ruach.

May His love flow in you and through you. May He fill you with compassion, patience, and understanding. May you bask in His Ruach HaKodesh (Holy Spirit).

Shalom,
Mama Ethel

"Do nothing out of selfishness or conceit, but *with humility consider others* as *more* important than yourselves"

Philippians 2:3

Chapter Eight

That Nasty Thing Called Pride

Why, oh why must we always be right? What is this driving force that makes us prove ourselves to the world? Yep, it's pride. And it's so hard to let it go!

Remember that wonderful verse in Philippians 2:3 that says, "Do nothing out of selfishness or conceit, but with humility consider others as more important than yourselves"—remember that?

Oy vey! Long ago in a galaxy far away, I once told my children, "It's more important to be loving and kind than to be right." They were wonderful words and I really wish I had practiced what I preached!

There was the day we were riding around in the car, and I saw the geese on the side of the road. "No," my young son said, "they're ducks!" The next 15 minutes consisted of a lengthy lecture by yours truly— after all, I had to prove that I was right! They were geese, of course!

There it is. It wasn't that important, but I HAD to be right. Does this sound familiar to you? This happens a lot in relationships, and maybe after reading this, you'll remember to think twice before you make the same mistake.

Husbands and wives do it all the time. It's almost comical to hear a couple get into an argument about the name of the very first Chinese Restaurant they ever visited, for example. Couples can go on this way for hours. When I hear arguments like this, I sometimes speak out and say, "Excuse me, but does it really matter?" (But inside I am screaming for them to just BE QUIET!)

Does it matter? If your wife or girlfriend says you met on a Tuesday and you just KNOW it was really on a Friday, DOES IT MATTER?

Of course, there are times when it is very important to be correct. If your doctor told you to take TWO tablets before bed and your spouse said, to take THREE, then please do get this straightened out ASAP.

Remember, when you are in a relationship, you should encourage the other person, not tear them down. It's just not nice to always find fault and always prove that you're right and they're wrong.

As I said in the beginning of this chapter, pride is a nasty thing. It causes us to think a bit too highly of ourselves. And you probably already know this, but when you're being self-centered, you're not being God-centered.

Whether you've been married for twenty-five years or whether you're in a brand new relationship, please remember that it really is more important to be loving and kind than to be right. If you've been struggling in this area, don't be too hard on yourself. Our God is a God of second chances and His mercies are new every morning. Today is a new day and it is filled with opportunities. And I'm right about that!

Mama Ethel

Be still,
and
know
that I am
God.
Psalm 46:11 (10)

Chapter Nine

Stop Trying to Fix People

I spoke with a young woman the other day who is in a difficult relationship. One moment the young man says he loves her, the next moment he retreats and slinks away. They already broke up once, and then six months later began again, although now it's a long distance relationship.

The same pattern is beginning again. I want to fix it and tell her to stop trying to fix him!

But wait! I need to trust God to help her, and she needs to trust God that He is in control and let Him deal with the young man. I'll call him Ricky and her Sarah.

My heart breaks for Sarah. She was rejected by her Dad as a baby; her first boyfriend/fiancé broke up with her; and now this.

I think I know what's going on here. When you are broken and you don't love yourself, you aren't able to love another. You can't really give of yourself when you are in need of emotional healing. Sarah needs this healing, and Ricky also obviously does. Until Ricky gets the help he needs, he won't be able to function in a healthy relationship.

I want to tell Sarah that it's not personal. It's not that she's not beautiful, lovable, and desirable—it's that he can't love her until he allows God to change him. And she herself needs to allow God to heal her heart also.

I know some of you are in unhealthy relationships now, whether married or single. It's so easy to be co-dependent and keep trying to fix the other person. We all do this. As long as we focus on fixing the other person, we don't have to focus on ourselves. We always want to control the situation, and we strive to make it work.

Had you ever heard the Scripture on page 46, "Be still and know that I am God"? It's Psalm 46:10 (46:11 in TLV). What does that really mean? It means slow down, take a deep breath, and give that steering wheel to God.

I don't know how long it's going to take. In Sarah's case I know she is hoping and praying that Ricky will come around. God can certainly change his heart. But Ricky has free will. He has to want to be healed; he has to want to change.

Sarah didn't ask me for my opinion and I didn't give it (as hard as that was)—I just told her I'd pray. I prayed for her and I prayed for Ricky, that he gets the healing that he needs so that he is free to love. Part of me just wants to tell her to run as far away from Ricky as possible, that she is just setting herself up for more heartache. But then she'd never know if Ricky was going to be healed. It's a risk she may want to take. She can hang in there, Ricky might end it—again, or he may be healed and finally be free to love her. By the time you finish this book it may have already resolved. I don't know God's timetable, of course.

I wonder how many times you've been in Sarah's situation? We all want so desperately to be loved and cherished. Sadly, we can't make someone love us. I truly believe that when it's of God, it comes easy—you don't have to struggle to make it work. It just flows.

If you are in a relationship with someone who is broken, encourage them to get the help they need, but don't try to fix them. You're not their mother, counselor, pastor, or rabbi.

Meanwhile, let's concentrate on fixing ourselves. How do we do this? It all comes back to our theme, "Hold fast to the Word." Surround yourself with uplifting people and let them know when you need prayer. Fellowship often with them. Listen to worship songs. Do all you can do to fight the good fight!

Two books that really helped me are *Women Who Love Too Much*[4] and *Codependent No More*.[5] Both books shed some light on what motivates us to want to fix others. The first book has interesting information on the types of men we select. It made me stop and think about a need I had to mother or fix others. If I always selected weak, needy men, then I was setting myself up for an unhealthy relationship. *Codependent No More* was a real eye-opener. While reading it, I realized that the failures and successes of my children affected me

---

4 Robin Norwood, *Women Who Love Too Much: When You Keep Wishing and Hoping He'll Change,* Pocket Book, a Division of Simon and Shuster, Inc., 1985, 1997, 2008.
5 Melody Beattie, *Codependent No More: How to Stop Controlling Others and Start Caring for Yourself,* ,Hazeldon Foundation, 1986, 1992.

much more deeply than they should. A codependent person is one who has let another person's behavior affect him or her, and who is obsessed with controlling that person's behavior.

At the end of the day it's all about trusting God, believing that He is in control, and our willingness to let go of the reins. It's good that you are concerned about your friends and loved ones. Pray for them and encourage them. However, if you lose sleep over their situation, if you dwell on it day and night, that's a warning that you are giving in to fear instead of trusting God.

Here's a good verse to memorize. May the Lord give you peace, dear ones!

Philippians 4:6-7 "Do not be anxious about anything—but in everything, by prayer and petition with thanksgiving, let your requests be made known to God. 7 And the shalom of God, which surpasses all understanding, will guard your hearts and your minds in Messiah Yeshua."

Mama Ethel

Because of the *mercies* of *Adonai* we will not be consumed, for His *compassions* never fail. They are new every morning! Great is Your *faithfulness*.

Lamentations 3:22-23

Chapter Ten

Hold Onto the Word

I was sitting across from my dear friend—I'll call her Susie. She was sad because she longs to be close to her sister who has rejected her. This feeling of rejection took root in Susie a long time ago and has kept her from feeling loved, cherished, and worthy in many of her relationships.

I thought about my own life and wondered how many times I gave in to depression and feelings of self-pity. I had a different upbringing from Susie, but I could still relate.

Recently I spoke at a retreat, and the theme was "Hold Fast to the Word." You know when we are holding onto lots of stuff, our arms get full. Ever try to carry too many grocery bags at once? You just don't have room for that one extra thing.

Many of us are holding on to fear, anger, unforgiveness, and self-rejection—just to name a few. We're so busy holding on to these negative attitudes that we have no room left to hold onto the Word of God.

I've learned a lot of things in my life so far, and one thing is for certain. The Lord loves us and wants us to lay our burdens down, rest our heads on His shoulder, and listen to His voice as He soothes us and speaks to our spirit. We just have to listen.

It's amazing what happens when we listen. I had just returned from a whirlwind trip to Virginia. My sister flew in from California, and we stayed with a friend. We visited our parents' graves and truly enjoyed being together. There was lots of laughter!

I was a bit anxious about being with my sister. After all, she is the older sister, has always been sarcastic and critical, not to mention, she's always been thinner, and never really had acne—and plays piano and guitar better than me.

The Lord had been gently speaking to me about my feelings toward my sister. Let's start with the jealousy/envy thing. That's really not very attractive, is it? How many times do we compare ourselves to someone else because we don't see ourselves the way God sees us? I have had to repeatedly repent of allowing this spirit of envy into my thoughts and had to replace it every time with the Word, which says in Psalm 139 that we are awesomely and wonderfully made.

I was expecting the worst. But if we expect there to be conflicts and worse, then we are already setting ourselves up to be angry, resentful, and bitter.

This was one of my God-downloads. I needed to go with an attitude of joy and acceptance, trusting God, expecting good things instead of bad.

Then God spoke to me about my need for attention. Ouch! My sister and I both come from a performance background. When God got ahold of me, I learned the difference between performance and worship. One gives glory to ME, the other gives glory to God. God reminded me that I needed to reflect Yeshua at all times. So that meant I needed to let my sister have the spotlight. Just sit back and let her be.

But wait—there's more! I also felt Him telling me that I needed to be the calm one on this trip. What? Me calm?! Ha! God certainly has a sense of humor now, doesn't He?!

He knew what He was talking about, because from the minute she picked me up from the airport, she pleaded with me—rather desperately—to sign up as an additional driver of the rental car. Richmond, Virginia isn't what it used to be, and after four attempts to find the airport, she was done with driving.

Again, God has such a sense of humor. Normally I ask OTHERS to drive because I don't like driving around in different locations. Usually I'm the one to panic. But not this time, and God had already prepared me.

Of course, I'm human, so I did slip once on this recent visit. My sister teased me in front of friends, and I got upset with her—in front of everyone. Later we both apologized and all is forgiven.

I share this experience with you because I want you to know that I understand what you're going through. I understand that it's not easy to take the high road, to be like Yeshua all the time. We slip up. We make mistakes.

Please forgive yourself when you mess up. His mercies and compassions are new every morning

(Lamentations 3:23). It's just as much a sin to harbor unforgiveness towards yourself as it is to hold on to it against others. He is faithful and just to forgive our sins when we are faithful to confess them.

At the beginning of this chapter, I mentioned my friend Susie. Maybe you have a friend like Susie, or maybe you're the one who suffers with abandonment issues, rejection, feelings of worthlessness, and self-pity.

It takes time but there is healing. As you grow stronger in your faith, as you spend more time in the Word, you become confident in your identity in Messiah. When you are confident, you don't take things personally. There's something freeing in that. Is someone rude to you? Don't take it personally. Is someone withdrawn, uncommunicative? Don't take it personally. Chances are, it has nothing to do with you. Pray for them. They are probably going through something. God knows.

Are you feeling lonely? Take the initiative—call someone. Are you bored? Take a walk, visit an art museum, or visit a nursing home and ask if there is someone who never gets a visitor. Go visit that person.

Sign up for a dance class, volunteer at your synagogue or church, or at your local library. In other words, take action. You may not feel like taking action, but if you go ahead, you may be pleasantly surprised how good you feel when you're meeting new people and being a blessing to others!

Of course, I am not saying that you can turn your emotions on and off like a light switch. Some people need extra help when dealing with depression, and I recognize that. Still I believe that we can renew our mind with the Word. There is power in the Word! God is the same yesterday, today and tomorrow—and miracles and healing still happen!

The enemy of our soul wants to cripple us. He knows if we hold on to fear, anxiety, anger, etc., then we will be immobilized, and won't be able to do God's work and further His Kingdom. Learn to identify the voices in your head. Resist the devil and he will flee (James 4:7)!

You know those pictures with the devil on one shoulder and an angel on the other? The devil is whispering in your ear, "You're ugly. You're an idiot. You'll never amount to anything. Everyone hates you!" And the angel of the Lord is on the other shoulder whispering, "You are a child of God. You are precious in His sight. You are beautiful. You are loved. There is a purpose and a plan for your life. You are smart and good. I dance for joy over you with singing" (Zephaniah 3:17). I ask you, which voice are you going to listen to? Who are you going to believe?

As I sign off, I just want to remind you to renew your mind (Romans 12:2) and be filled with peace. Remember, when you hold onto His Word, you will stay strong. When you hold onto His Word, you are refreshed. And you will learn to listen to only His voice.

Mama Ethel

"Master, how often shall I
forgive my brother
when he sins
against me?
Up to seven times?"

Yeshua said to him,

"No, not up to
seven times,

I tell you, but
seventy times seven!

Matthew 18:21-22

Chapter Eleven

Forgiveness

Shalom mischpochah! Let's talk about forgiveness—or shall I say the lack thereof....

We know the Bible says that we are to forgive seventy times seven (Matthew 18:22). Some have said that forgiveness is conditional—we can only forgive if the other person repents. Others have said we are to forgive always, under all circumstances.

Whoa! Hold on there, pardner. I didn't say it was easy. But it could be worse. Thank God I have never had to forgive someone for murdering a loved one, and I hope you haven't had to deal with such a horrible thing either. That would be extremely difficult. I can't even imagine the pain and suffering that would bring. Through prayer and counseling, I'm sure it would slowly get better, but it would take a long time to heal from something that tragic.

However, that being said, some of us have been deeply wounded, whether by friends, family members, or loved ones. We have been betrayed and have endured lies, deceit, and worse. I am not suggesting that we just shove it under a rug and forget about it, but I am saying that with God's help we must learn to forgive. Others may disagree, but I say, yes, forgive, EVEN IF THEY DON'T APOLOGIZE OR REPENT. When we hold on to a grudge or harbor anger, it does something to us. Our bodies often suffer from the pain of bitterness. It can definitely affect our physical and mental health.

Studies have shown that those with the highest levels of anger are twice as likely to suffer with heart disease or stroke. In addition, there can be problems with digestion, anxiety, insomnia, headaches, high blood pressure, and depression.

Someone once said that holding on to anger and bitterness is like taking poison and waiting for the other person to die.

Ephesians 4:25-27 says, "So lay aside lying and 'each one of you speak truth with his neighbor,' for we are members of one another. 26 'Be angry, yet do not sin.' Do not let the sun go down on your anger, 27 nor give the devil a foothold."

In our relationships with our families and loved ones, we can easily be wounded. In arguments, we tend to bring up the past and go into the "He said…she said" routine, where we mention all the past grievances and do all that we can to undermine and belittle our sparring partner.

1Cor.13:6-7 says, Love "...does not rejoice over injustice but rejoices in the truth; 7 it bears all things, it believes all things, it hopes all things, it endures all things."

Forgiveness

My brothers and sisters, as hard as it is, choose to forgive, choose to love! Ask the Lord to help you, to give you supernatural love for the one that has wronged you. You may not want to do it, but every day, say a prayer for that person, ask the Lord to bless them. In this way, you will free yourself from all bitterness and anger that you have held toward this person. If you know you are holding onto anger, repent, and renounce it, resist it, and remove it in the Name of Yeshua!

I know a little bit about the affects of unforgiveness. Many years ago I was hurt deeply. I met "Norman" through the mail. Before computers, before online dating, there were pen-pals. A friend gave me his address, said he was in the Navy and lonely and asked that I write to him. After nine months of exchanging thoughts on everything from world hunger to favorite movies, we met in person, and I knew he was the one.

After a brief courtship, we married. I left the security of my mother's house and entered the unknown. I had never been in a relationship before. I tried my best to please him. He often found fault with me, but I tried harder and harder to win his approval and his love. It worked to a tolerable degree.

Seven years later we started our family and our relationship began to worsen. I couldn't go out with him like before, and he didn't like to stay home. Arguments increased. I often cried myself to sleep. No matter what I did, I couldn't please him anymore. He was unhappy and restless. Still, I had hopes. I would just try harder, and things would get better.

Chapter Eleven

But in the autumn of 1985, my bubble burst, and my life became the plot of a sad country western ballad. That's when my husband left me, and I was alone with my two toddler sons, my baby daughter, a deaf dog, and a cat. How could this be happening? I could barely get out of bed each morning. Never had I felt so alone. I was absolutely terrified.

No family lived nearby and I struggled for air as I drowned in a sea of despair. Sadness turned into bitterness and hatred. Not only did I hate him for leaving, I hated the situation, and I hated myself. I also hated the other woman. I was mad at the whole world.

I did my best to hide my misery from the children. As I tucked them into bed each night and stroked their hair, I prayed that I would have enough money to pay the bills. I prayed that their winter coats from the previous year would still fit their ever growing bodies. I was terrified that the utility companies would turn off my heat and electricity.

Yes, money was tight. At first we didn't even have a car. Later my dear sweet mother helped me buy a used lemon—I mean—car— so at least I could drive to the store. Grocery shopping was always a challenge. I had my two darling boys, one on each side of the cart, and my baby daughter inside the cart in her car seat surrounded by soup cans and diapers.

It was embarrassing to go on food stamps and enroll in the WIC (Women Infants & Children) program. I'm sure the children grew tired of macaroni and cheese, peanut butter and jelly sandwiches, and ramen noodle soup.

I looked for shoulders and arms that would hold me up as I fell deeper and deeper into anxiety, bitterness and unforgiveness. How could I forgive the one who shot an arrow directly into my heart? How could I forgive the one who betrayed me, who left me and our children?

I was holding on to a grudge. I was taking that poison and waiting for the other person to die. Bitterness and unforgiveness were the poison, and I was consuming mass quantities on a daily basis. Would I ever be able to let go of my anger?

Then I met Daniel. No, I could not bring this poison into a new relationship. With the help of friends, through many prayers, and sessions with some wise counselors, I learned to let it go. This doesn't mean it didn't afflict me with attempts to re-enter my heart, but little by little I made the decision to forgive.

It was the most difficult decision I ever made. But it was also the best. By deciding to forgive, I had truly made the best decision of my life.

I could now enter a new relationship with Daniel without bringing in any poison. Now I could continue on my journey with a smile on my face and love in my heart.

In marriage especially, you must "choose your battles." The Lord has given me wisdom many times and helped me make the right decision when Daniel and I have had our differences. The bottom line—my relationship with my husband is more important than holding on to anger towards him. We may be upset for a short time, but neither of us holds on to unforgiveness towards the other.

You may be thinking, "Well, you don't know what I've been through. It's much worse than what you experienced. You can't possibly understand." That may be true. I am certainly not suggesting that you stay in an abusive relationship or put you or your children in danger. I am simply saying, that no matter what has happened, in time, with God's help, learn to forgive, learn to let go of the anger.

Sadly, even as believers, we often hurt one another. Let us try to live according to the words in our Bible: Micah 6:8 says, "He has told you, humanity, what is good, and what ADONAI is seeking from you: Only to practice justice, to love mercy, and to walk humbly with your God."

May the Lord give you His supernatural strength to forgive anyone who has hurt you, and may you walk in His shalom!

Mama Ethel

"I, Adonai,
called You
in righteousness,
I will take hold
of Your hand,
I will
keep You...."

Isaiah 42:6

Chapter Twelve

Triggers

Do you sometimes find yourself over-reacting when a loved one suggests an alternative approach, or corrects you? Did one of your parents correct you often, leaving you hurt, angry, and resentful? Without realizing it, we often react very strongly at times because we have some unresolved issues.

It's helpful to ask the Lord, "Why am I reacting this way?" For example, when my husband repeatedly rearranges the dishwasher and shows me a more "efficient" way, I find myself angry. When I stop and analyze it, I am remembering my childhood and how I felt when my Dad corrected me. He always had a better way of doing everything, and I felt inadequate every time he showed me his "better way."

It's very hard to admit this, and it makes me aware that more inner healing is needed. Part of the healing for all of us is to remember to see ourselves as God sees us. Psalm 139 says we are "awesomely and wonderfully made." And again there are many more Scriptures (too many to list) that remind us that we are loved and that God cares for us so very much.

Remember that quote from before—"expectations are planned resentments." As we saw, it's true when we have high expectations for the best, but it's also true when we expect the worst. If you expect someone to hurt you, disappoint you, criticize you, etc., then you are already preparing to resent them. It's really hard to stay positive, but remember that, as believers in Yeshua, we can renew our minds by focusing on the Word. And we need to keep in line with the Golden Rule. I would not like it if someone expected the worst from me. Would you like it?

Sometimes people can surprise us and treat us far better than we expected. I spend far too much time assuming the worst, but I am often surprised and delighted when things go well. We should strive to think positively about people. They might even live up to our expectations! But if not, let's not resent them.

No matter how old we are, we are still learning, still growing, and gradually still healing from our early wounds. The important thing is to recognize these triggers, and when they happen, to ask the Lord to show us where it's really coming from. Perhaps we are holding on to resentment toward our parents or someone in our past, and we need to allow the Lord to heal us.

If we find ourselves often angry, then we need to repent of allowing a spirit of anger to operate in our life. We need to resist that negative spirit, renounce it, and remove it and the root cause of it in the Name of Yeshua, and replace it with an infilling anew of the Ruach. It's not easy to remove it, but just as perfect love drives out fear (1 John 4:18), God's Spirit in us drives out negative emotions that rob us of our peace and joy.

And as I've stated before, I am not an expert on relationships. I just like sharing the things I've learned along the way. It's a good reminder for me, too.

To sum up the things I've mentioned before, here are "Mama Ethel's" rules for having successful relationships:

- You can't truly love another unless you love yourself.
- Don't try to be "right." Focus on being loving and kind.
- Don't take things personally.
- Listen more, talk less.
- Focus on the positives.
- Expect the best, not the worst.
- Choose your battles. If it's not life and death, let it go.
- Forgive yourself and others.

There will be more items to add to the list as we go on. Remember, God's mercies are new every morning, and each day that you wake up, you have an amazing opportunity to make a difference and be a blessing!

Mama Ethel

Speaking the truth
in *love*,
we are to grow up
in all ways
into *Messiah*,
who is the Head.

Ephesians 4:15

Chapter Thirteen

When You Disagree

No matter how many times you laugh, hug, and snuggle, sooner or later you are going to disagree. And I hope you do. Wait, what? Yes, you certainly need to know how to disagree with each other. It's part of all relationships! If someone is always saying "yes, dear," then that someone is not being true to themselves.

When you disagree, do you have to fight? No! There is a way to disagree peacefully. First of all, let your partner talk and really listen. Don't interrupt! Find out why they think what they think. Use reflective listening skills, i.e., "So what you're saying is…….." Go back and read Chapter 4 again ("Is Anybody Listening" page 25) to help you listen and reflect well, so they will feel heard and understood.

Finally, when they are done, it's okay to state your point of view, but do it without criticizing or condemning them for their opinion. Don't belittle them, or speak angrily. Just kindly and gently express how you feel, and say why.

Chapter Thirteen

Sometimes you need to peacefully agree to disagree. Too many times we let anger get in the way. We use sharp, abrasive tones and hurtful words and make our partners feel badly for their thoughts. It is better to lovingly seek to understand the way the other person thinks—to find out where they're coming from..

It's perfectly okay to disagree. Just be respectful and kind. Always.

Mama Ethel

"...we are more than conquerors through Him who *loved* us.
... [nothing] will be able to separate us
from the *love* of God that is in
Messiah Yeshua
our Lord

Romans 8:37, 39

Chapter Fourteen

Know You Are Loved and Act Accordingly

This had been on my mind a lot, and I gave this advice to at least three people in the month before writing this. Earlier in Chapter 9, I talked about the importance of loving and accepting yourself, so you are free to love and be loved. It's not easy to do. So many times we are disappointed and angry with ourselves.

To recap, we must learn to see ourselves as God sees us. And as we confess our sins and receive His forgiveness, we must also forgive ourselves.

As you read the Word over and over, you'll see multiple reminders that God loves you, accepts you, and promises to never leave you. One of my favorites is Romans 8:37-39 "But in all these things we are more than conquerors through Him who loved us. 38 For I am convinced that neither death nor life, nor angels nor principalities, nor things present nor things to come, nor powers, 39 nor height nor depth, nor any other created thing will be able to separate us from the love of God that is in Messiah Yeshua our Lord."

I always tell people that one of the many reasons for reading the Bible over and over is so we are constantly reminded of these promises. Reading these wonderful Scriptures again and again is one way to get the message planted deep into your soul, your heart, and your brain.

Yet how many times do you doubt? Maybe you're doubting right now. Maybe you don't think you are really forgiven, and don't believe that you are loved. This puts you on a dangerous slippery slope, my friend. If you doubt God's love, then my guess is that you also doubt the love of your friends and family. This is such a sad condition.

There are two scenarios that I want you to imagine. The first scenario is this: You walk into a room, and you already know that the people inside the room do not like you. They don't accept you, they think very little of you, and they constantly mock you. The room is dark and cold, and smells a little musty. You feel trapped. It's hard to breathe, and you are ashamed and full of dread. You don't dare look anyone in the eye, and no one seems to look at you either. It's as if you don't exist. You leave as soon as possible, gasping for air as you exit the room.

Now, here is the second scenario: You walk into a room and expect that everyone in the room likes you. You know this deep within your spirit. The room is bright, cheerful, and warm. You are greeted warmly. You feel like hugging everyone, and they hug you back! There is laughter and music, and even the air smells sweet. There is no fear, no shame, or despair, only love, acceptance, and joy. You could stay in this room forever. (It kind of makes me think it will be like this in Heaven!)

I would like to propose that whenever your are facing an uncomfortable experience, whether it is a job interview or you are walking into a family reunion, that you always imagine scenario 2. If you imagine scenario 1, then you are already expecting and planning to be shunned and disregarded.

Yes, unfortunately, there will be times when people don't warm up to us. There's always someone out there that doesn't like us, but in my experience, in most cases, when we smile and look them in the eye, they smile back.

Those of us who are familiar with Gary Chapman's book, *The Five Love Languages*, know that people express love in different ways. The five languages in the book are:

1. Words of Affirmation
2. Acts of Service
3. Giving Gifts
4. Quality Time
5. Physical Touch

This is where we often fall short when it comes to our close friends or families. We start to question whether or not we're loved. We imagine something similar to scenario 1. We assume that we're not loved or valued. When this happens, please try to take a step back and think about how your loved ones express love to you. It may be that "acts of service" is their love language. So they just love to do things for you. Maybe your love language is "words of affirmation," and when you don't get those encouraging words from people, you start to doubt that you're loved.

My hope and prayer for you is that you notice that you ARE loved. We have already established that God loves you very much. It says so in His Word over and over. When you really stop to think about it, your family and friends love you too! Know that you are loved and act accordingly!

Love ya,
Mama Ethel

Man
looks at the
outward
appearance,
but *ADONAI*
looks into
the heart.

1 Samuel 16:7

Chapter Fifteen

You Are Beautiful

One of my favorite stories is "The Velveteen Rabbit" by Margery Williams. It's an adorable story about a conversation between a rabbit and a skin horse. The rabbit asks the skin horse, "What is real?" As we read their discussion, we learn that you become real when you're loved for a long time, and that by then, generally "most of your hair has been loved off," and you "get loose in the joints and very shabby." The wonderful conclusion is that once you're real, you "can't be ugly, except to those who don't understand."

Unfortunately, we live in a society that is obsessed with the outward appearance. We are bombarded with advertisements on TV, in magazines, and on the internet that lead us to believe that once you are thin enough, have the right clothes, house, car, and makeup, then you'll be successful and happy.

I love what the Bible has to say on the subject, "Man looks at the outward appearance, but ADONAI looks into the heart" (1 Samuel 16:7). So I'd like to ask you this question: How many people have you avoided or rejected because you didn't like their looks? If we're honest, we will realize that at some point in our lives, we've all done it. It's easier to smile at an attractive person, especially one who dresses nicely and smells nice also. Perhaps you were one of those overweight kids who never got picked for a team—you know what I'm talking about. Sadly, it's not just children who practice this cruel form of rejection. It's us adults, too.

Growing up in Richmond, Virginia, my sweet Mama used to say to me, "Are you beautiful because I love you or do I love you because you're beautiful?" I always concluded that it was because she loved me.

What about you? Do you have someone in your life that thinks you're beautiful? In chapter nine, I said that you couldn't really love another unless you loved yourself. It's hard to love yourself when you don't like what you see in the mirror, or when you've been repeatedly hurt by others.

I want to ask you another question: Are you willing to see yourself as God sees you? He really does think you're beautiful. In Zephaniah 3:17 it says that He will dance over you with singing. He loves you and in His eyes you are absolutely stunning! You can hold your head up high because you know that you are adored, accepted, approved, and loved by the Almighty God!

My children often heard me say, "It's more important how you act than how you look." Of course, we must do our part to keep clean, well groomed, and to dress modestly. The important thing is not to be obsessed with our looks, like so many are. Seek to please the Lord each day, dress for Him! You don't have to have clothes from Macy's or Lord & Taylor. I've seen beautiful clothes from many thrift shops.

Men, this addresses you as well as the ladies. Focus on becoming more like Yeshua, and you will shine. People will be attracted to the light—to His light. Isn't that what you want?

And remember, every child of God deserves to be treated with respect. The next time you pass someone on the street who seems a little disheveled, look at her and smile! It doesn't cost anything to bring joy into another's life. When you pass a worker, whether it's the janitor at the office or the construction worker outside, greet him and say, "Keep up the good work!" You will make their day!

I know many of you out there are single and hoping to meet that special someone soon. While physical attraction is certainly part of the equation, please don't overlook the wonderful personalities that God has put before you. You may be pleasantly surprised that the short man with crooked teeth is the kindest, most Godly person on the planet. The woman with frumpy clothes and braces may have a ministry that totally matches what God has put on your heart. Keep your eyes and ears open to what God is saying to you. Seek Him first and He'll guide you!

You're beautiful because He loves you!
Mama Ethel

"By this all
will know
that you are
My disciples,
if you have
love
for one another."

John 13:35

Chapter Sixteen

Please and Thank You

It sounds so simple to say those two little words, yet we so easily forget them as we go through our daily routines. We're pretty good at remembering to show proper respect for our peers and colleagues outside of the home, but what about for our spouse and children or our housemates or college roommates?

Let's think about how you feel when you're treated disrespectfuly. When asked for a favor or to do a task, the tone of voice matters. If someone says, "Bring me my slippers," doesn't it sound like an order from a commanding officer? But what if they were to kindly say, "Honey, would you please bring me my reading glasses?" Doesn't that make you feel a whole lot better? So be sure to ask that way, and then when you thank them, everyone feels better!

There's a song that says, "They'll know we are Christians (Messianic Jews, believers, whatever word you want to use) by our love." [6] One of the best ways to show love to each other is to treat each other with kindness at all times.

6 "They'll Know We Are Christians" written by: Regie Hamm, Daniel Mucka-la, Peter Scholtes; album: Rise up and Sing 3rd Edition, Vol. 5, released: 2009.

Chapter Sixteen

Unfortunately, there are too many TV shows and movies out there that show a distorted view of relationships. The writers and directors are constantly flaunting dishonest, unfaithful, and hurtful people who are filled with rage, and mistreat others with their lies and controlling behavior. It saddens me to see people flocking to the movie theater to see such filth. I am concerned that we are exposed to such atrocities.

As believers in Messiah, we must show the world what true love is. When we are filled with the gifts of the Spirit and demonstrate these gifts in our daily interactions, we are flooding the world with the light of Yeshua.

If you took a survey from those who are happily married, you would find that the happiest couples are those who consistently treat each other with respect and kindness. Not only do they say "please" and "thank you" but also "I love you" many times a day. And many couples still hold hands, no matter how long they have been married.

In Proverbs 16:24 it says, "Pleasant words are honeycomb—sweet to the soul and healing to the bones." There is much wisdom in that statement. And this goes way beyond our homes. When we are at the bank, the grocery store, or even the DMV, we often find ourselves having to wait in line behind a very rude customer. Or the teller or cashier is having a particularly challenging day and is being too slow or has to call a manager. During these moments, you have a choice. You can still respond with kindness and love, or you ⁓ allow yourself to be caught up in the web of chaos.

I would like to suggest that you take a moment in these situations and breathe in Shalom! Shalom, as you know, is the greeting in Hebrew for "hello" or "goodbye" that means "peace," but did you know that it also means "to destroy the authority of chaos?" Let God's Shalom wash over you in all situations. As we let the Ruach fill us to overflowing, we will destroy the authority of chaos!

I especially need to remember this when driving on the road. When other cars cut me off or tailgate me, I don't always remember to breathe in that wonderful peace, and the result is an anxious spirit, an angry attitude, and knots in my stomach. At times like this, I would be better off taking deep breaths and asking the Lord for help. There, I have confessed one of my weaknesses. I feel better already. Now I just need to put my own advice into action.

Remember, you don't know what people are going through. Everyone handles stressful situations differently, and sometimes, without meaning to, someone may explode in anger or react rudely when it has absolutely nothing to do with you. It's hard to not take things personally, but it's better if you remember that most likely, it's not about you. Pray and try to extend grace. How many times has our Father in Heaven extended grace toward us?

Sometimes you need to do a reality check. As I was preparing this article, I asked my husband, "Honey, do I treat you with respect? Do I say please and thank you enough?" He said I did. That made me happy, but since I'm not perfect, I know I have to work on this and not ever take him for granted.

In summary, let's remember to show respect and kindness towards everyone, to not take anyone for granted, and to extend grace and forgiveness often! Please? Thank you!

Blessings,
Mama Ethel

**God
has not given me
a spirit of fear
but of power and of love
and of a sound mind.**

2 Timothy 1:7 (NKJV)

Perfect love drives out fear.

1 John 4:18

Chapter Seventeen

Perfect Love Drives Out Fear

Shalom mishpocha! I've been writing a lot about relationships. As I said in my intro, I am not an expert. I've just "been around the block" a few times and have learned a lot along the way. In the past few chapters I've shared how you really can't love another person until you love yourself, and then there was a discussion about pride and having to prove that you are always right.

In this chapter, I thought I'd talk a little bit about fear. Fear and I go way back, not that I'm very proud to admit it. Fear is one of the most crippling enemies of our soul, and it causes us to become paralyzed and ineffective in the Kingdom of God. The enemy knows that if he can keep us locked up in fear, we won't be winning souls for Messiah.

Those of us who give in to this wicked spirit spend an awful lot of time worrying about things that will never happen. We imagine the worst-case scenarios and suffer from everything from insomnia to high blood pressure to heart trouble to other physical ailments.

Fear can certainly ruin a perfectly good relationship. If you are always suspicious of your spouse or partner, if you imagine their death every time they are five minutes late, or are constantly worried that he or she might leave you, then we have a serious problem.

Perhaps you're one of those people who tremble when visiting the doctor because you're sure that every headache is a brain tumor, every cough is lung cancer, and every stomach pain is diverticulitis. I hate to admit it, but I've been guilty of this many times.

Where did all your fear come from? Was there an "entry point" or a specific time in your past when you remember first feeling afraid? According to Henry Wright, author of *A More Excellent Way,*[7] fear is a spirit and after we recognize it in ourselves, we must take responsibility for allowing it in our minds. We must repent, then renounce it, resist it, and remove it in the Name of Yeshua! Then daily we need to replace the fearful thoughts with words from Scripture, like "Perfect love drives out fear" (1 John 4:18), or "God has not given me a spirit of fear but of power and of love and of a sound mind" (2 Timothy 1:7 NKJV). And we must "take every thought captive and make it obey the Messiah" (2 Cor. 10:5 CJB)!

Those who work in the medical profession will agree that most people with high blood pressure are those who worry and have anxiety.

---

7 Henry W. Wright, *A More Excellent Way: Be in Health: Pathways of Wholeness, Spiritual Roots of Disease*, Pleasant Valley Publications; 1st edition 1999, 7th edition, 2005.

So what can we do? We must daily renew our mind with words from Scripture (Romans 12:2). And we must take deep breaths. Remember, with God's help you can control your thoughts. Instead of imagining that your loved one was just in a car crash, practice trusting God. Know that He is watching over them. Remember, when Yeshua was in the desert, He was bombarded by the enemy, and He overcame him with the Word! The Word of God is our weapon! There is a popular praise song called, "The Battle Belongs to the Lord." [8] Hallelujah!

And know that you are loved! Perhaps you are also dealing with the fear of abandonment or the fear of rejection. Again, take responsibility over those thoughts and rebuke them in Yeshua's Name. Don't listen to the lies of the enemy. See yourself as the Lord sees you. You are a daughter or son of the King of Kings! My dear friends, "He will not fail you or abandon you" (Deuteronomy 31:6). He "will never leave you or forsake you" (Hebrews 13:5).

I am so much happier when I am walking in peace. When I am at peace, it spills over to my relationships on the job and at home with my family.

I know that you can't turn feelings on and off like a light switch, and that I haven't experienced all the same things you have. However, I do know that holding on to fear and anxiety will keep you from experiencing joy.

After my first husband left us, I was feeling very unloved and was full of doubt and fear. Would anyone ever love me again? Would someone want a woman

---

8 Jamie Owens-Collins © 1985 Fairhill Music (Admin. by Fairhill Music, Inc.)

with three little children (even though they were adorable!)? Was I damaged goods? How would I ever survive on my own? I had no experience in this department. I went directly from my parents' house to an apartment and a husband. I didn't even know how to cook. I barely knew how to boil water.

Daily chores were a struggle. I stood at the sink washing dishes, staring out the window, tears streaming down my face. Why did he leave? Was I such a horrible person? I kept looking for personal flaws. Maybe I didn't listen well enough. Maybe I nagged too much. Or worst of all, maybe I just wasn't pretty enough! How could I go on with my life?

I had been put down so much that I started to believe that I was horrible. Yet somehow I knew that I had to learn to love myself, so I could be whole and healthy again. Until I was able to love myself, I would not be able to receive love from anyone else. This was so difficult! I needed some help. I surely didn't want to stay in this dark place where I was afraid of my own shadow. I needed to grab onto faith—I had to believe that God loved me and had a plan for my life, and that somehow, with His help, we would survive.

Eventually, I found solace at a few Bible studies, and began to regularly attend Friday night services at Congregation Brith Hadoshah (New Covenant in Hebrew) in Buffalo, New York. Slowly, cautiously, I made new friends and learned to laugh again. I learned to see myself as God sees me, and started to like myself for the first time in a long time. Praise the Lord.

Coming to personally know God's perfect love for me began to drive out my fear.

Sometimes it helps to talk things over with someone. We all need to be validated, to feel that we are understood, to know that someone cares. Talk to your Messianic Rabbi or Pastor, or, if you like, you can seek professional help. The important thing is that you share your feelings with someone. That's what I did.

I also had to fight off fear about entering a new relationship. Should I open up my heart once more? Wasn't it too risky?

I met Daniel on my first visit to Congregation Brith Hadoshah. We chatted a bit after service, and I remember asking him to please pray for my marriage because things weren't very good at that time. Several months later, I found myself a single parent with three small children.

After I later began to regularly attend Brith Hadoshah every Shabbat (Sabbath), I learned that Daniel was a janitor. I mistakenly assumed that meant he wasn't very bright, but was quickly proven wrong when I started attending the adult Shabbat school, similar to Sunday school. He was brilliantly teaching the class! I later learned that he was working full-time as a janitor while also attending graduate school full-time.

I found him to be funny, intelligent, and humorous. He even teased me a little bit, which I enjoyed. We became friends, and I noticed how wonderfully attentive he was to my children, and how well they responded to him. Six months after we first got acquainted, he called and asked if I would go out with him. Remember my strange response? I said, "Well, I wouldn't exactly be repulsed!"

We had a few dates alone, but most of our time was spent doing things with the children. One night he was visiting me at my house, and he put the children to bed for me. As he came down the stairs, he said, "Ethel, I have a confession to make."

All I could think about was, "What?! Did you steal the silverware?"

He said, "I'm in love with your children!"

After dating for nine months, on the last night of Hanukkah, 1987, he presented me with a rolled up document, similar to a diploma. As I unraveled it, I began to see that it looked like a Ketubah, a Jewish wedding contract. When I saw the words where he pledged to love me forever, I asked, "What is this?"

He said, "I'm asking you something!"

Suddenly I realized it was a proposal and said, "YES!!!" We immediately told the children, but they were immersed in Hanukkah wrapping paper. They responded with excitement later.

By the following summer, August, 1988, we stood together under the chupah (canopy) and pledged our love in marriage. And it's been a wonderful journey ever since! He even took my mother in when she was at the beginning stages of Alzheimer's, and I had the same opportunity to help care for his mother several years later. And now we have received the awesome privilege of becoming grandparents to two amazing little darlings. God has truly blessed us!

However, as I began my second marriage, I had to battle fear again. Would my new husband grow tired of me also? Would he love me just as I am or would I have to conform into an upgraded model? When he was momentarily annoyed or cross, did that mean he no longer loved me?

One day I was in one of my "pity parties," and I started thinking that maybe my husband didn't find me attractive anymore. The next day I found a dime on the ground. I felt the Lord prompting me to pick it up, tape it to a post-it note, and stick it on the refrigerator as a reminder that my husband thinks I'm a TEN! (The best score!) Now whenever I have doubts or worries about my husband's thoughts, I just look at that post-it note and smile!

We're all going to have good days and not so good days. Just remember that His mercies are new every morning (Lamentations 3:23). If today didn't go so well, just shake off the dust and try again tomorrow. There are countless opportunities every day. As long as we don't let fear control us, we "can do all things through Messiah who strengthens" us (Philippians 4:13). As you put off fear, anxiety, and worry, you will be happier, your relationships will blossom, and your joy will overflow!

Can somebody say "Amen"?

Mama Ethel

Love
one another
fervently
from
a pure heart

1 Peter 1:22

Chapter Eighteen

The Power of Hugs

Shalom my friends! Lately the Lord has got me thinking about the importance of touch—specifically hugs! Most people like to give and receive hugs. Something happens to us when we are hugged. Our breathing slows down, our blood pressure drops, and our whole body relaxes. We feel accepted, loved, and peaceful.

Studies have shown that babies don't thrive when touch is withheld. Some of us are afraid to touch or be touched, because it is often misunderstood. We live in an age where we question motives and mistrust those who want to touch our arm, squeeze our shoulder, or hug us.

Have you ever observed people in a church or synagogue? There is usually a greeting time where folks shake hands or hug. It's interesting to sit back and observe the way people interact. There are those who give the full bear hug, holding nothing back. Other folks stand a few feet apart and gently pat the other person on the back, as if to say, "I'll let you hug me but only for a second!" Then there are those who turn sideways and hug for a few quick moments, careful to avoid close contact. Still others hug for a VERY long time, and you squirm uncomfortably, waiting for a moment to break free.

Some people are afraid to let others hug them because in that moment they become vulnerable, and they might cry. Let's face it, some of us long to be hugged, and the loneliness can be overwhelming at times. When we are finally hugged, the dam just breaks. Sometimes we just can't control it.

Those of us who are married or in a relationship forget that there are many people who don't receive hugs on a regular basis. We need to be sensitive to those who don't have a hugger in their life. Maybe it's the mother in me, but if I had my way, I'd hug each of you for a very long time, every day.

In the Scriptures, there are vivid images of Yeshua touching others with fabulous results of healing—both physical and mental. Sometimes we need to close our eyes and visualize Yeshua reaching out to us! Imagine His wonderful hugs and the power of His touch! When He hugs us, we are instantly cleansed, refreshed, and filled with His peace and joy! I am at peace just thinking about Him in this way.

However, having said all this, we must also respect that there are those who don't want others to touch them. Some people do not like to be hugged and are very uncomfortable when others invade their personal space. I always like to ask someone, "Is it all right if I hug you?" If they say, "Yes," then I give them a great big "Mama Ethel" hug, because, after all, that's what I do!

I just want to encourage you to seek the Lord and be sensitive about touch. Know when it's alright to reach out and touch someone. Find out if they would rather you hold their hand, pat their back, or hug them, and what kind of hug they like. As brothers and sisters in Messiah, and especially in relationships, we should encourage and reassure others in the same way that we would like to be encouraged. When you extend your hand or hug someone the way they prefer, you are telling them that they are valued, important, special, and most of all, loved.

If I had my way, we would have a national holiday dedicated to hugging, at least once a month—or better yet, daily. People are so good about remembering their daily doses of vitamins, medications, and fiber, but sometimes we all forget that a hug a day keeps the doctor away! Hug your family, your friends, and even your pets. Hugs are good for you, just like your veggies are!

Love and hugs,
Mama Ethel

Let no harmful word come
out of your mouth,
but only what is

beneficial

for building others up
according to the *need*....

Ephesians 4:29

Chapter Nineteen

Let's Do Lunch

I love meeting new people and getting to know them. I especially appreciate those times when I was new in the area, and others reached out to me and my family, having us in their homes and making us feel welcomed.

In this chapter, I want to address the importance of saying what you mean and meaning what you say. How many times have you met the new family in town and without thinking, blurted out, "We should get together sometime," or "I'd love to have you over for dinner sometime"?

Did you really mean that? I remember one occasion when I had moved to a new area. I began attending the local Messianic congregation, and a few families were very friendly. One family mentioned a few times that it would be loads of fun to have us over sometime. I felt so excited to think that someone wanted to get to know us.

Three years later....we did get invited and had a wonderful time. I don't mention these things just to hold a grudge and mull over bad memories, as I've forgiven them. However, I do want to encourage you to be careful with your words.

The same rule applies when you say, "Hi, how are you?" If you really don't want to know the answer, please don't ask the question.

Did you tell someone that you'd call them and then forget to call? Did you promise to make a lunch date with someone and then break that promise?

Also, how many times do we say, "I'll pray for you," and then we forget? How would you feel if someone promised to pray for your situation, only to find out that they never once thought of you and went on their merry way?

As a Jewish mother, I have lots of practice inflicting guilt, but I assure you that guilt is not the motivator for this chapter. I just want to remind you that it's important that we are genuine with people and sensitive to how they might be feeling.

It's really pretty simple. The next time you say, "We should do lunch," make a date right then and there. And when you say, "I'd love to have you over for dinner sometime," find a date and time and book it on your calendar.

When you say you'll pray, PRAY! Offer to pray with the person immediately, if possible, or write it down so that you'll remember.

What are the benefits of keeping our word and following through? When we honor our word, we are pleasing to the Lord. We also gain a reputation for being sincere and genuine. Taking the time to get to know new people is rewarding and exciting and inspires trust.

You may be thinking that you're way too busy to have people over or to go out on lunch dates. If that's true, then stop hinting at making such plans. If you know you really won't do it, don't say it! Just be true to your word. Only you know your schedule and your time limitations.

If God is leading you to open your home or to make lunch plans, then He will help you find the time. The third chapter of Ecclesiastes tells us that there is a time and a season for everything.

Oops, gotta go! Time for lunch!

Mama Ethel

Guard your heart
diligently,
for from it
flow
the springs
of *life.*

Proverbs 4:23

Chapter Twenty

Just Friends

There's one last topic I want to address. It is the answer to a question I often get asked. The question is: **Can a man and a woman be just friends?**

The short answer is "No!" Here's why I think that. Men and women are often lonely and seeking companionship. They long to enjoy movies, nature, and Indian food with someone, laugh together and hug. But there's also that thing called "chemistry."

We are both physical and emotional beings. While it's possible for someone to be asexual and not ever desire physical intimacy, most of the time one or both parties is attracted to the other person. For the woman it might be more of an emotional attraction, and for the man it may be a sexual attraction. Of course, it can be the other way around, too.

You may be friends for a long time, but sooner or later, one or both parties will be attracted to the other. Sometimes this leads to a wonderful romantic relationship, one that is based on true friendship. That is a desired outcome, for sure! Some of the best marriages are ones that were based on this kind of friendship.

I do think it is a bit naive to think that you can hang around with a guy or gal without them ever being attracted to you. I know a lot of guys who like having female friends. Sometimes these guys are emotionally damaged and don't let themselves love another. (Maybe they don't love themselves and aren't really able to love anyone else.) But their female friends love being with them and want more. Ultimately the ladies are devastated to learn that their male friend just wasn't capable of loving them. And then the women move on, heartbroken.

A point of clarification. This is crucially important, so pay attention. If someone is married, they should not continue to be close friends with someone of the opposite sex unless their spouse is included. It's very dangerous to share your deepest thoughts and feelings with someone other than your spouse. An emotional affair can easily turn into a physical affair.

I know women who have lots of guy friends and they just don't get it. Of course the guys are going to be attracted to you. Wake up!

Okay enough said. I know many will disagree with me but again, this is my opinion based on my real life observations.

Mama Ethel

What is impossible with man *is possible* **with God.**

Luke 18:27

Chapter Twenty-One

The Conclusion of Mama Ethel's Marriage Advice

So you've come to the end of the book. I realize not every chapter deals with a love relationship. Some chapters address how we treat others that we encounter whether in church, synagogue, at work, etc. You probably heard most of the advice before, so think of this as a gentle reminder. Love yourself, respect others, don't worry about being right, etc. Read this book over a few times until it all sinks in.

Relationships are hard work, and sometimes you will make mistakes. Just be sure to say, "I'm sorry" often and always strive to meet the other's needs above your own.

Forgive each other, and forgive yourself. Remember that His mercies are new every morning!

A while back, I made this short list. It's my own little marriage advice list:

1. Pray together every day.
2. Never go to bed angry.
3. It's more important to be loving and kind than to be right.
4. Find something encouraging to say to your spouse every day.
5. Think before you speak.
6. Put your spouse's needs first.
7. Always say I'm sorry.
8. Laugh often.
9. Show appreciation daily.
10. Respect each other.

This short list and the principles in the rest of this book have served Daniel and I very well. Our love for the Lord and for each other has been going strong for 35 years! And we anticipate many more! We are very blessed.

May the Lord bless you and guide you. May He fill you with peace, joy, and lots of patience!!! I have faith in you, dear one. With God's help nothing is impossible!

Luke 18:27 "What is impossible with man is possible with God."

Mama Ethel

**They overcame him
by the**
Blood of the *Lamb*
and by the
word of their
testimony,

Rev. 12:11

Chapter Twenty-Two

My Testimony

I was born in Richmond, Virginia to two Jewish parents. I was the youngest of two girls. We were Holiday Jews, attending synagogue only for Rosh Hashanah (the Jewish new year) and Yom Kippur (the day of atonement). My parents sent me to Hebrew school for five years, where I learned to read and write Hebrew.

My mother had a very strong faith in God, and taught me to recite Psalm 23 whenever I was afraid. Later, during my teenage years, I was drawn to the occult, especially astrology. I was always searching for something, but didn't know what.

A few experiences made an impact on me. Once when riding a bicycle down a tree lined street, I noticed one tree taller than all the rest, and the thought popped into my head that the taller tree was like Jesus overlooking His disciples. But I scolded myself because a nice Jewish girl doesn't think about Jesus. After all, I was taught that He was just a prophet, and that we Jews, didn't believe He was the Messiah. We considered it blasphemous that He would think Himself to be like God. So it was really uncharacteristic of me to think about Jesus at all.

I sang Christmas carols in school, but never really knew what I was singing about. Even when I sang Handel's "Messiah," I never realized that those were words that came out of the book of Isaiah, and that they were prophesying about the true Messiah.

Later, when I graduated from high school, there was a pastor on stage with the principal when a few of us received a special citation. The pastor had been there to do the opening invocation, and came around to each of us to shake our hands when we received our citations. When he came to me, he looked deep into my eyes and said, "You will do great and mighty things for our Lord." I was so uncomfortable and couldn't wait for him to go to the next person.

In the fall of 1972, I went to college for a year, majoring in music education and voice. The president of the music club was a Christian and invited me to a meeting where people were sharing their testimonies. I attended out of curiosity, but was really scared and turned off. He gave me a tract that said, "Jews for Jesus." I was so afraid of it that I just crumpled it up and threw it in the garbage can. I guess I wasn't ready yet.

One day a friend approached me and said she had a cousin in the Navy, and he wanted to write to a nice Jewish girl. I said, "Okay." As I said earlier, we wrote for a few months, and I met him when he got out of the Navy. It was a whirlwind romance. I dropped out of school. I was no longer interested in pursuing a music degree. I just wanted my "MRS" degree.

We got married in March 1974, and lived in New Jersey for our first year of marriage. His company moved us to Rochester, New York in the spring of 1975, and that's where my spiritual journey really began. I got a job working as a typist at Eastman Kodak, and Doreen, the girl next to me, had a picture of Jesus on her desk and read her Bible at lunch. My husband and I argued a lot, and I cried a lot. I was really drawn to Doreen because she seemed to have the peace that I was lacking. She gently began to share snippets with me, and I found myself curious, so much so that I opened the New Testament for the first time in my life!

Most Jews will never look at a New Testament because they think that it's anti-Semitic. I was so surprised to read about king David on the very first page, and to see the genealogy. As I read other pages, it struck me that it was such a Jewish book!

I was really touched by the beatitudes. I thought that the words of Jesus were life-giving and beautiful. Doreen introduced me to a Jewish believer at work who invited me to a Bible study where they were celebrating Passover. I began to see the symbolism and to understand that Jesus said He came to *fulfill* the law and the prophets not to *change* them (Matthew 5:17).

In July, 1976, I asked Jesus, Yeshua as I now call Him, to come into my heart. I wasn't sure if I had become a Christian and was no longer Jewish or what I had done, but it was the beginning of a beautiful journey. I learned later that I had not converted to another religion, but that I was now a completed Jew or Messianic Jew. I like to say that Jesus made me kosher.

There's so much more to my story. Suffice it to say that through all the trials and tribulations, God has been with me every step of the way, and I am a truly blessed woman.

One very interesting blessing is that even though I never got my degree in music, the Lord has given me opportunities to lead choral workshops at many Messianic retreats and conferences, and I have sung and played piano in many congregations. And I continue to be involved in music ministry today.

Psalm 40:4 has become my life verse since I'm a worship leader, and I sing all the time:

Psalm 40

1 For the music director, a psalm of David.
2 I waited patiently for Adonai.
He bent down to me and heard my cry.
3 He brought me up out of the slimy pit,
out of the mud and mire.
Then He set my feet on a rock.
He made my steps firm.
4 He put a new song in my mouth—
a hymn of praise to our God.
Many will see and fear,
and trust in Adonai.

**Every word of God
is pure;
He is a *shield*
to those who
put their *trust*
in Him.**

Proverbs 30:5

About the author

Ethel Chadwick lives in Western New York with her husband, Daniel, and adorable cat, Roxy. They raised three wonderful children together and have two sweet grandchildren. Daniel is an online faculty for several colleges and universities. Ethel enjoys retirement by dancing, singing, and playing piano. She currently hosts the popular Messianic Radio Show "Bagels and Blessings" and is the Worship Director at Congregation Shema Yisrael in Rochester, New York.

Ethel gives all glory and praise and the highest thanks to Adonai Yeshua first and foremost. She also wishes to thank her friends for their love and support and most of all she appreciates the wonderful encouragement she receives from Daniel.

They recently celebrated thirty-five years of marriage and look forward to many more years together!

Comments and questions are welcomed! Send an email to bagelsandblessings@gmail.com.

May you be filled to overflowing ...

... with God's perfect Love.